FLOWERS AND THEIR MEANINGS

A SMALL BOOK ON FLOWERS, TO HELP YOU CHOOSE THE BEST FOR YOUR BEST MOMENT

SANA TANDON

"To my Best Friend, who always supported and encouraged me."

Contents

CHAPTER ONE

Blue Bells

Enter Caption

Hyacinthoides non-scripta is a bulbous perennial plant, found in Atlantic areas from north-western Spain to the British Isles, and also frequently used as a garden plant.

Meaning-

These bell-shaped blooms represent kindness. They're also perfect gift to show someone how grateful you are for their love, friendship and support

CHAPTER TWO

Aster

Enter Caption

Aster is a genus of perennial flowering plants in the family Asteraceae. The name Aster comes from the Ancient Greek ἀστήρ meaning 'Star', referring to the shape of the flower head.

Meaning-

Based on Victorian culture, Aster embody daintiness and charm. Greek mythology lovers will also be interested to know that they can be a symbol of Love.

CHAPTER THREE

Cosmos

Enter Caption

Cosmos is a genus, with the same common name of consisting of flowering plants in the sunflower family. These are native to scrub and meadowland in Mexico where most of the species occur. In the USA, some varieties maybe found as far north as the Olympic Peninsula in Washington, but the range also extends through Central America and South America.

Meaning-

With its orderly arrangement of petals, its only natural that cosmos b known for Order and Harmony. There are several colors to choose from including different shades of Pink, Purple, Red and Orange.

Yellow Rose

Enter Caption

Rosa 'Golden Celebration' is Yellow shrub rose cultivar, bred by British Rose Breeder, David C.H Austin.

Meaning-

Based on its meaning, you might second-guess gifting this rose color to a loved one. Yellow roses have a hidden symbolism of jealousy and infidelity. However gifting them to a friend can mean Warmth and Affection

CHAPTER FIVE

Delphinium

Enter Caption

Delphinium is a genus of about 300 species of perennial flowering plants in the family Ranunculaceae, native throughout the northern hemisphere and also in the high mountains of tropical Africa.

Meaning-

Officially known as the 'birth flower of july', Delphiniums are gifted for encouragement and joy. Different colors have different meanings- Blue Delphinium symbolizes dignity and the White, Pink and Light blue represents youth and renewal

CHAPTER SIX

Freesia

Enter Caption

Freesia is a genus of Herbaceous perennial flowering plants in the family Iridaceae, first described as a genus by Christian Friedrich. It is native to Eastern side of Southern Africa, from Kenya to South Africa, most species being found in Cape provinces.

Meaning-

Freesia are popular for their citrus fragrance and long-lasting vase life. Gifting someone a bouquet of Freesia may symbolize Friendship along with innocence, purity and trust

CHAPTER SEVEN

Cala Lily

Enter Caption

Zantedechia is a genus of eight species of herbaceous perennial flowering plants in the family Araceae. They are native to Southern Africa from South Africa north to Malawi.

Meaning-

Do you find someone beautiful (inside and out)? Give them a bouquet of Cala Lilies to represent your attraction. Unknown to some, the true flower is the spike on the inside, while the outer petal is a leaf.

CHAPTER EIGHT

Hyacinth

Enter Caption

Hyacinth is a small genus of bulbous, spring-blooming perennials. They are fragrant flowers in the family Asparagaceae. They are native to the area Eastern Mediterranean from South Turkey to Israel.

Meaning-

This bloom is dedicated to Greek Sun god Apollo. They signify games, sports and play. You can give this flower to someone who loves to play sports as a way of encouragement for an upcoming game.

Gladiolus

Enter Caption

Gladiolus is a genus of perennial cormous flowering plants in the Iris family. The genus occurs in Asia, Mediterranean Europe, South Africa and tropical Africa.

Meaning-

Integrity, strength and victory are the meaning for these blooms (also known as August Birth flowers). Gift these 'flower of Gladiators' to recent graduate or game winners

CHAPTER TEN

Marigold

Enter Caption

Tagetes of annual or perennial, mostly herbaceous plants in the family of Asteraceae. They are native to the Americas, growing naturally from the Southwestern United States to South America.

Meaning-

Marigold are beautiful gifts for someone in mourning or stricken grief. They also have a hidden meaning of jeaoulsy.

• 13 •

CHAPTER ELEVEN

Tansy

Enter Caption

Tansy is a perennial, herbaceous flowering plant in the genus Tanacetum in the aster family. They are native to temperate Europe and Asia.

Meaning-

Although tansies are common additions in bouquets, they at times can be declaration of war. In other occasion they an symbolize protection and hope for good health (as their name comes from Greek word for Immortality)

CHAPTER TWELVE

Lotus

Enter Caption

Nelumbo nucifera, also known as Indian Lotus, sacred Lotus or simply Lotus is one of the two extant species of aquatic plants in the family of Nelumbonaceae. It has a very wide native distribution ranging from central and northern India, through northern Indochina and East Asia with isolated location at Caspian sea.

Meaning-

These flower grow in the mud. Each night they return to mud and then miraculously re-bloom in the morning. In many Eastern cultures they signify re-birth, self- regeneration, purity and enlightenment.

CHAPTER THIRTEEN

Carnation

Enter Caption

Dianthus caryophyllus commonly known as Carnation or Clove pink is a species of Dianthus. It is probably native to the Mediterranean region but its exact range is unknown due to extensive cultivation for last 2000 years.

Meaning-

These ruffly flowers may be the stuff of high school secret admirers but they work for a lover on a budget. If you pick one these blooms choose White ("sweet and lovely") or pink ("I'll never forget you"). But stay away from other colors.

The two-tones versions means "I cannot be with you" and yellow ones signify "disdain".

CHAPTER FOURTEEN

Magnolia

Enter Caption

Magnolia is a large genus of about 210 flowering plant species in the subfamily Magnolioideae of the family Magnoliaceae. It is named after French Botanist Pierre magnol. The natural range of magnolia species is disjunct distribution, with a main center in East and Southeast Asia and a secondary center in Eastern North America, Central America and West Indies.

Meaning-

These stunning blooms often festoon the trees as spring arrives, getting everyone who sees them excited for the season to come. That's why its only logical that they signify a love of nature.

Dahlia

Enter Caption

Dahlia is a genus of bushy, tuberous perennial flowering plant. They are native to Mexico and Central America.

Meaning-

When you hear the name, you probably think of black Dahlia. Well never fear. These ruffled flowers stands for Dignity and pomp, so they would feel right at home at a momentous occasions like graduation or new job

CHAPTER SIXTEEN

Iris

Enter Caption

Iris is a genus of 260-300 species of flowering plants with showy flowers. It takes its name from the Greek word for a rainbow, which is also the name for the Greek goddess of Rainbow, Iris. It is found in temperate northern hemisphere zones, from Europe to Asia and across North America.

Meaning-

These regal blooms have long stood for royalty, but also for wisdom and respect. And there opulent-looking blooms sure suggest the same. That means its definitely a compliment if you receive a bouquet of Irises.

CHAPTER SEVENTEEN

Red Tulip

Enter Caption

Tulips are a genus of spring-blooming perennial herbaceous bulbiferous geophytes. Mainly found from Southeast Europe and Turkey in the west.

Meaning-

Red roses aren't the only flower with a romantic meaning, so you don't have to totally splurge to show your dedication. Red tulips are also considered a declaration of Love and they especially gorgeous in the spring

Salvia

Enter Caption

Salvia is the largest genus of plant in the sage family *Lamiaceae* with nearly 1000 species of shrubs, herbaceous perennials and annuals. They are distributed throughout the old world and the America's.

Meaning-

Depending on its color Salvia can have several different meanings. Blue salvia (like this one) means "thinking of you" but in red it means "forever mine".

CHAPTER NINETEEN

Edelweiss

Enter Caption

Leontopodium nivale commonly called edelweiss is a mountain flower belonging to the daisy or sunflower family. It is a scarce short-lived flower found in remote mountain areas.

Meaning-

The sound of music fans already know the song, but did you know the meaning behind it? Edelweiss stands for courage and devotion, probably because they thrive in harsh Alpine conditions.

CHAPTER TWENTY

Myrtle

Enter Caption

Myrtus with the common name Myrtle, is a genus of flowering plant in the family of Myrtaceae. It is native to Mediterranean region in Southern Europe.

Meaning-

If you need the perfect bloom to add to a wedding bouquet, look no further than Myrtle. It stands for good luck and love in marriage, so there's no better flower to carry down the aisle